Cat's Cradle

A Book of String Figures

by Anne Akers Johnson

KLUTZ

KLUTZ® creates activity books and other great stuff for kids ages 3 to 103. We began our corporate life in 1977 in a garage we shared with a Chevrolet Impala. Although we've outgrown that first office, Klutz galactic headquarters is still staffed entirely by real human beings. For those of you who collect mission statements, here's ours:

Create wonderful things • Be good • Have fun

Book and string made in Korea. 91

Write Us
We would love to hear
your comments regarding this or
any of our books.

KLUTZ®
557 Broadway
New York, NY 10012
thefolks@klutz.com

Distributed in the UK by
Scholastic UK Ltd
Euston House
24 Eversholt Street
London, NW11DB
United Kingdom

Distributed in Australia by
Scholastic Australia Ltd
PO Box 579
Gosford, NSW
Australia 2250

Distributed in Canada by
Scholastic Canada Ltd
604 King Street West
Toronto, Ontario
Canada M5V 1E1

Distributed in Hong Kong by
Scholastic Hong Kong Ltd
Suites 2001-2, Top Glory
Tower
262 Gloucester Road
Causeway Bay, Hong Kong

Distributed in Europe by
Scholastic Ltd
Unit 89E, Lagan Road,
Dublin Industrial Estate,
Glasnevin, Dublin 11
Ireland

ISBN 978-1-878257-53-6

8 9 8

MIX
Paper from
responsible sources
FSC www.fsc.org
FSC® C023083

We make Klutz books using resources that have been approved according to the FSC® standard which is managed by the Forest Stewardship Council®. This means the paper in this book comes from well managed FSC®-certified forests and other controlled sources.

About String Games

A s long as there's been string, people have played string games. All over the world, people have amazed each other by turning an ordinary piece of string into a picture of something out of their everyday lives. The Arctic Inuit made reindeer and wolves out of string, while the Navajo knew how to make coyotes and owls. These string pictures were also used to help in the telling of stories and legends. Sometimes the figures were so complicated, people had to use mouths and toes as well as all ten fingers. But don't worry. You won't have to work so hard at any of the figures in this book.

Just as you'd suspect, most grown-ups around today have completely forgotten how to make the Witch's Broom or Jacob's Ladder. Your job is to show them how it's done. So go on. Find a quiet corner and practice making the figures in this book until you're good. Really good. Then round up your friends and family and dazzle them.

You'll do best if you start at the beginning of the book with some of the easier games. If you get stuck, try reading the instructions out loud. It helps.

Cup and Saucer

1 Start by looping the string across both of your palms and behind your pinkies and thumbs.

2 Now reach across with the first finger of your right hand and pick up the string that runs across the left palm.

***Red* means "This is the next piece of string you'll pick up."**

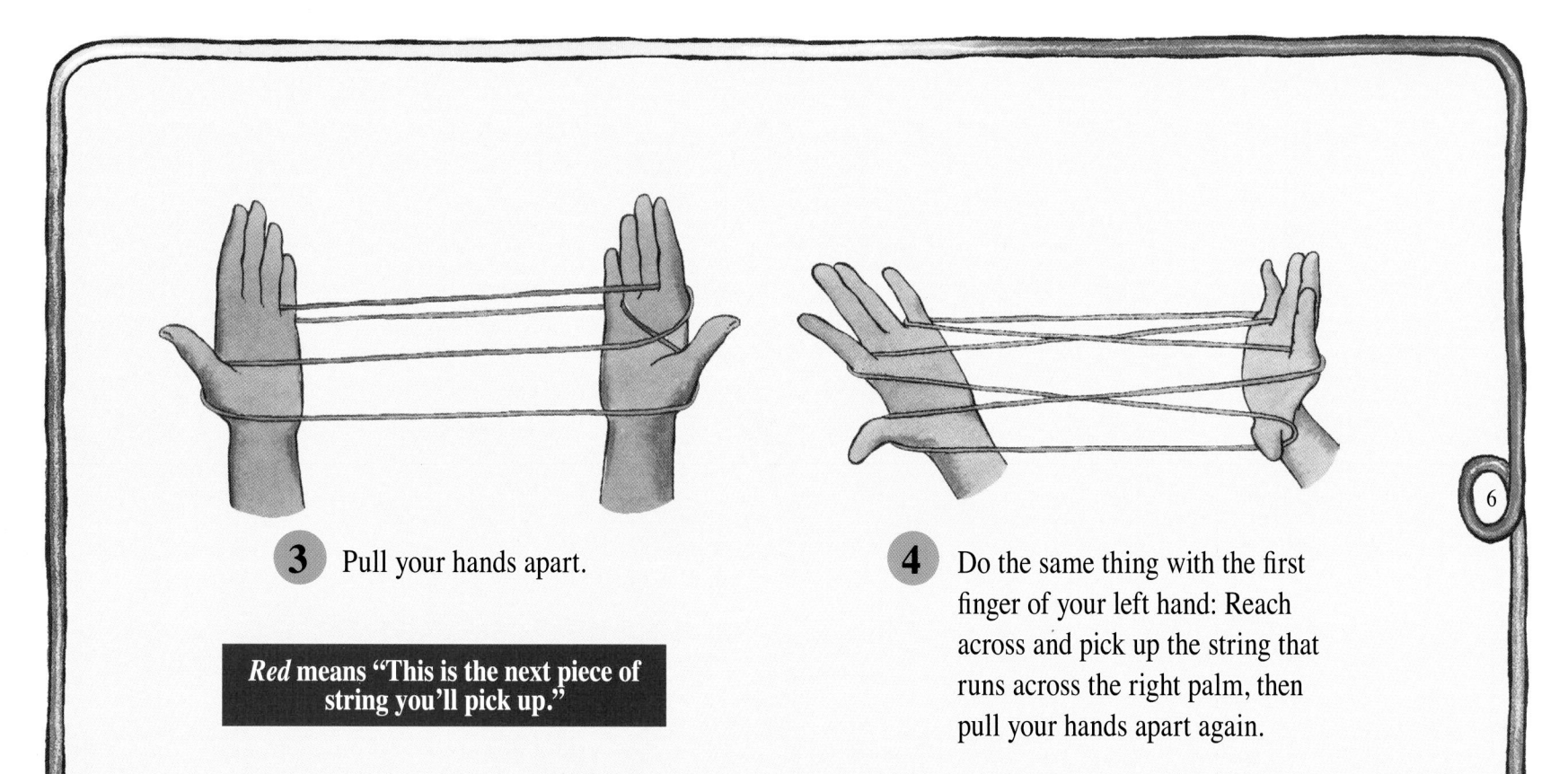

3 Pull your hands apart.

Red means "This is the next piece of string you'll pick up."

4 Do the same thing with the first finger of your left hand: Reach across and pick up the string that runs across the right palm, then pull your hands apart again.

6

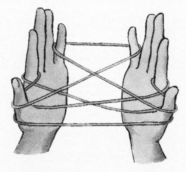

5 Now reach over both thumbs and hook them under the string on the far side of each first finger. Look at the picture: It helps.

6 Pull your thumbs back to where they started from. You'll have two loops on each thumb.

7 Using your mouth or your other hand if you can, pull the bottom loops off your thumbs. These loops will have to pass over the top ones to come off.

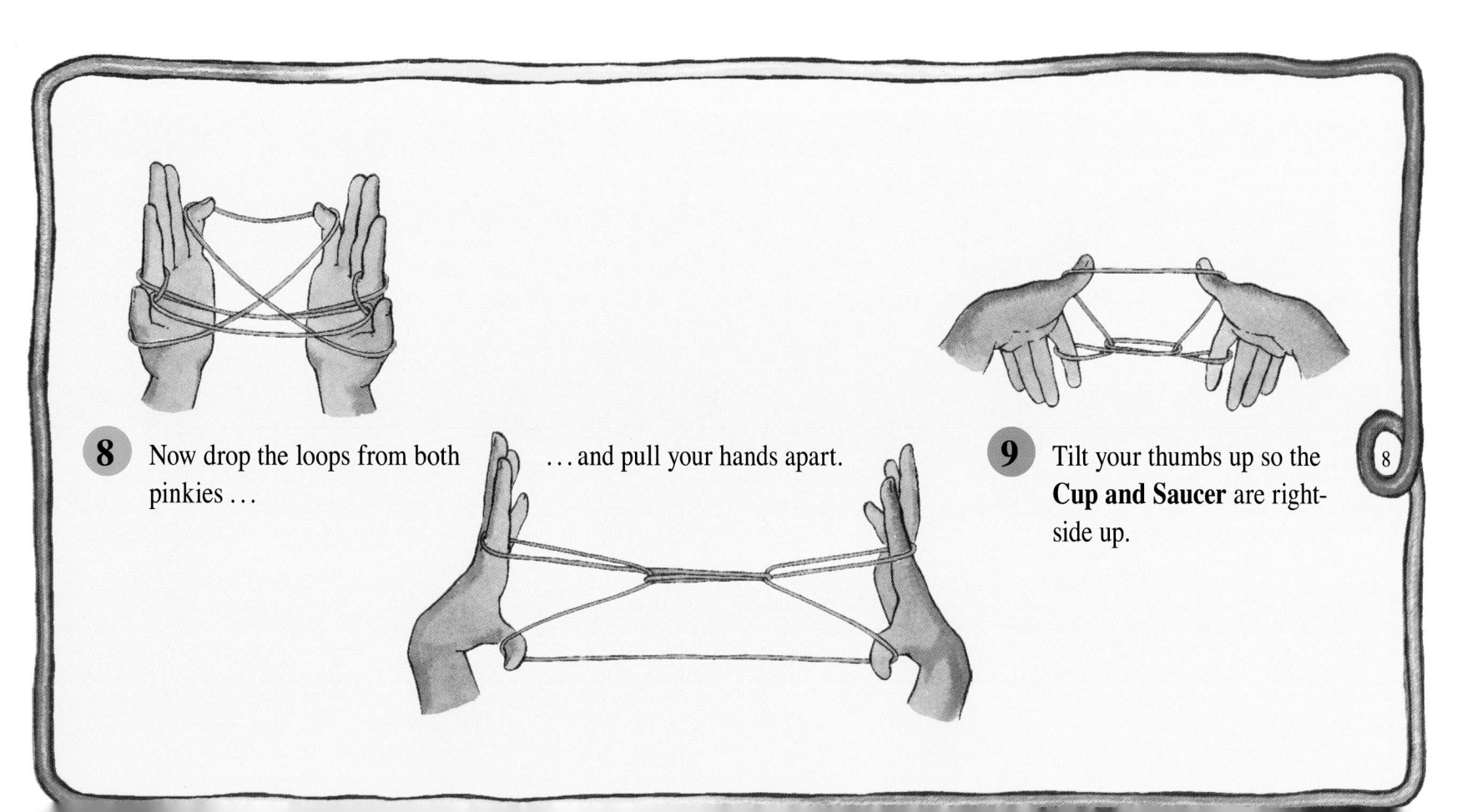

8 Now drop the loops from both pinkies ...

... and pull your hands apart.

9 Tilt your thumbs up so the **Cup and Saucer** are right-side up.

Eiffel Tower

1 Start with a **Cup and Saucer.** Catch the string that makes up the top of the cup in your teeth …

2 …then drop the loops from your thumbs, and pull your hands down gently. Don't pull the strings too tight, or it won't work.

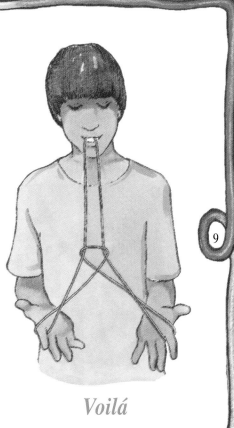

Voilá

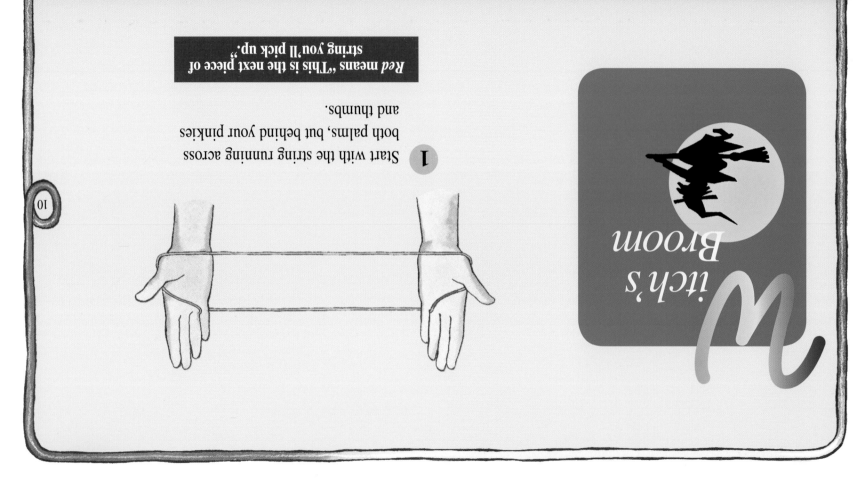

M
Witch's Broom

1 Start with the string running across both palms, but behind your pinkies and thumbs.

Red means "This is the next piece of string you'll pick up."

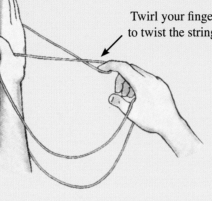

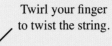

Twirl your finger to twist the string.

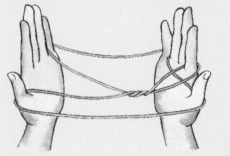

2 Reach across with the first finger of your right hand and hook it under the string that runs across your left palm. Don't pull your hands all the way apart yet.

3 Twist this new loop twice by twirling your first finger around twice . . .

4 . . . then pull your hands apart.

5 The next step is to reach across with your left first finger and catch the string that runs across your right palm. The trick is to reach through the loop you've just twisted to pick up the string.

6 Pull your hands apart again.

Red means "This is the next piece of string you'll pick up."

7 Drop the loops from the thumb and pinkie of your right hand and pull your hands apart so the strings are tight. There's the **Witch's Broom**.

12

Cat's Cradle

This is a string game that take two people to play so find a friend to help you out. You'll be the first player and your friend will be the second. It will be easiest if you put the book down between the two of you with the red arrow pointing at you and the blue arrow at your friend.

First player:

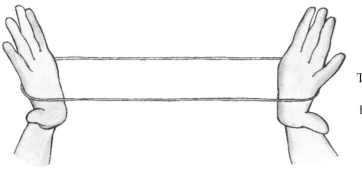

This time the string goes behind your hands.

1 Start by looping the string around the fingers of both hands. Leave your thumbs out of the loop.

2 Now loop it around both hands once more so that it wraps around the back of your hands twice and crosses your palms once. Look at the picture for help.

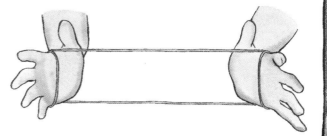

3 Reach across with the middle finger of your right hand and catch the string that runs across your left palm. Pull your hands apart.

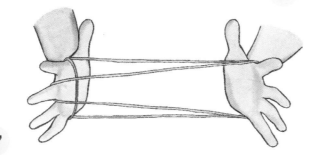

4 Do the same thing with your left middle finger. Reach across and hook under the string that crosses your right hand. Pull your hands apart. You've just made the **Cat's Cradle.** Now you can rest while your partner takes a turn.

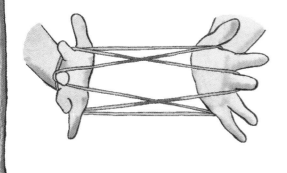

Second player:

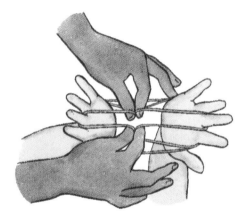

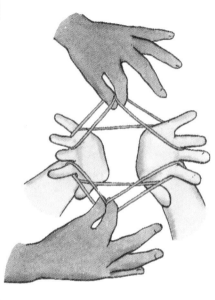

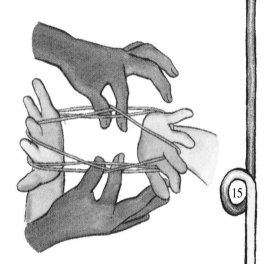

 Look straight down on the string in your friend's hands and you'll see two **X**s. Pinch the **X**s right where they cross.

2 Keep pinching the **X**s and pull them out past the side strings like the picture shows.

3 Turn your hands over and push your fingers (still pinching!) down outside the side strings then up into the open center.

15

From the Soldier's Bed to Candles

First player:

1 Okay, now it's your turn to look for the two **X**s. You're going to do pretty much the same thing your partner just did.

Pinch the two **X**s right where they cross …

2 …pull them out over the outside strings …

4 Pull your hands apart, and at the same time have your partner drop the strings so her hands are free.

This is called the **Soldier's Bed.**

16

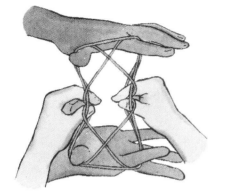

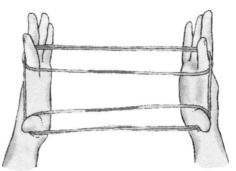

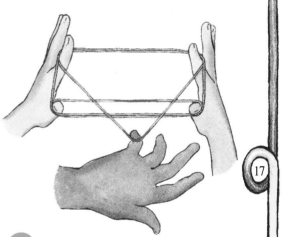

Second player:

3 ...then duck your fingers under the outside strings and push them up into the open center.

4 Pull your hands apart at the same time that your friend drops the strings from her hands. Now you've made **Candles**.

1 This one's a bit different, but not hard. Find the two strings marked in red. Use your right pinkie to hook the left string. Pull it way out over the outside strings and hold it there.

Red **means "This is the next piece of string you'll pick up."**

17

2 Next, hook the other red string with your left pinkie. Pull it out over the outside string. If you look down on the string, you'll see you've made two little triangles.

3 Hold these pinkie strings tightly and turn your hands over so the palms face down. Pinch the thumb and first finger of each hand together and push them down into the triangles, under the outside strings . . .

4 . . . and up into the center.

Red means "This is the next piece of string you'll pick up."

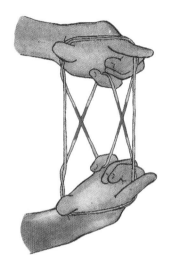

First player:

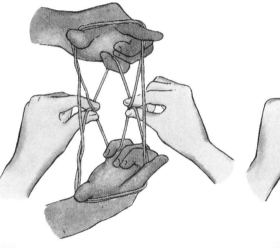

5 Keep holding the pinkie strings tightly and spread your thumbs and first fingers apart as you pull your hands apart. While you do this, have your partner drop the strings from her hands. This is the **Manger**.

1 Look down on the strings and find the two **X**s again. This time you're going to pinch the **X**s from the outside.

2 Pull these strings out past the straight outside strings and pull them up.

19

4 Spread your fingers and pull your hands apart at the same time that your partner lets go of the string. Now you've made **Diamonds**.

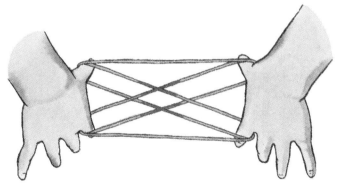

3 Still pinching tightly, turn your hands over and push your pinching fingers down into the open center.

Red means "This is the next piece of string you'll pick up."

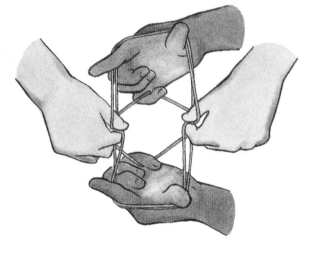

Second player:

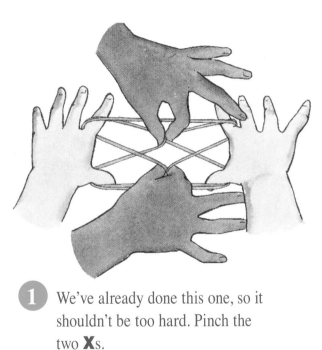

1 We've already done this one, so it shouldn't be too hard. Pinch the two **X**s.

2 Lift them out over the outside strings ...

21

3 ...then duck your fingers under the outside strings and up into the center.

4 Spread your fingers and hands apart at the same time that your friend drops the string from her hands and **you've got the Cat's Eye.**

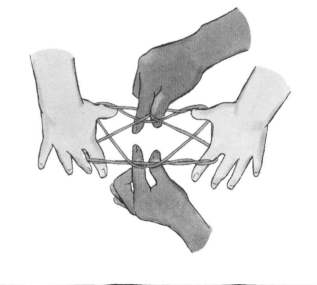

First player:

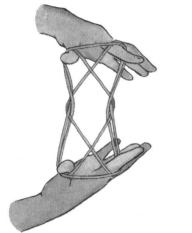

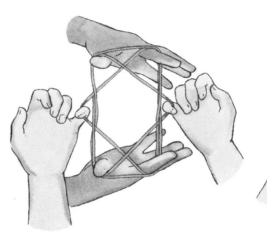

1 Now it's your turn for something a little trickier. Look at the strings carefully and find the two loops we've marked in red. They each make a short loop around the outside strings.

2 Hook your pinkies into these loops from underneath ...

3 ...and pull them out wide to make two little triangles.

Red means "This is the next piece of string you'll pick up."

23

4 Be sure you've got a good grip on these pinkie strings. Turn your hands over and push the thumb and first finger on each hand down into the triangles under the outside strings and up into the center.

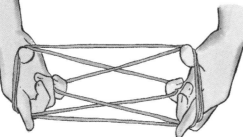

5 Now pull your hands apart and spread your fingers while your buddy drops the string. You're back to the **Manger.**

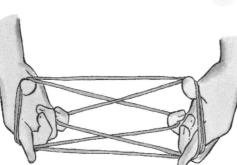

Go back and find the directions for the **Manger** (on page 19) and keep playing. This time you'll be doing all the steps your partner did the first time through. It will probably be easier if you turn the book so that the other arrow is point at you now.

Jacob's Ladder

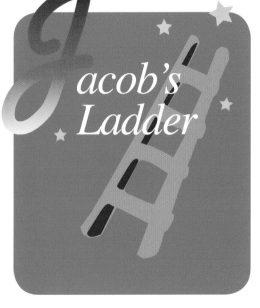

1 Loop the string across both of your palms and behind your pinkies and thumbs.

2 Reach across with the first finger of your right hand and hook the string that runs across your left hand.

Red means "This is the next piece of string you'll pick up."

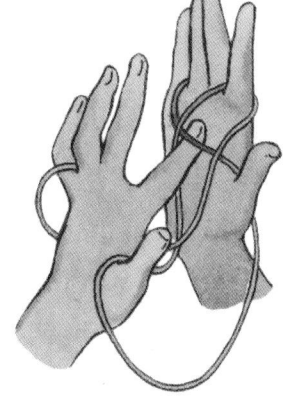

3 Pull your hands apart.

Red means "This is the next piece of string you'll pick up."

4 Do the same thing with the other hand. Reach over with your left finger and hook the string that runs across your right palm.

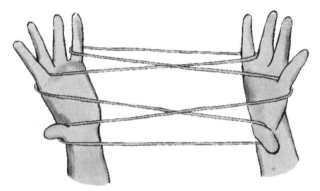

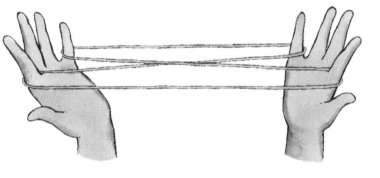

 Pull your hands apart so the string is pulled tight.

 Drop the loops off your thumbs.

7 Reach your thumbs under all of the strings so they hook the farthest-away string from the outside.

Red means "This is the next piece of string you'll pick up."

8 Pull this string back under all the others and spread your fingers apart.

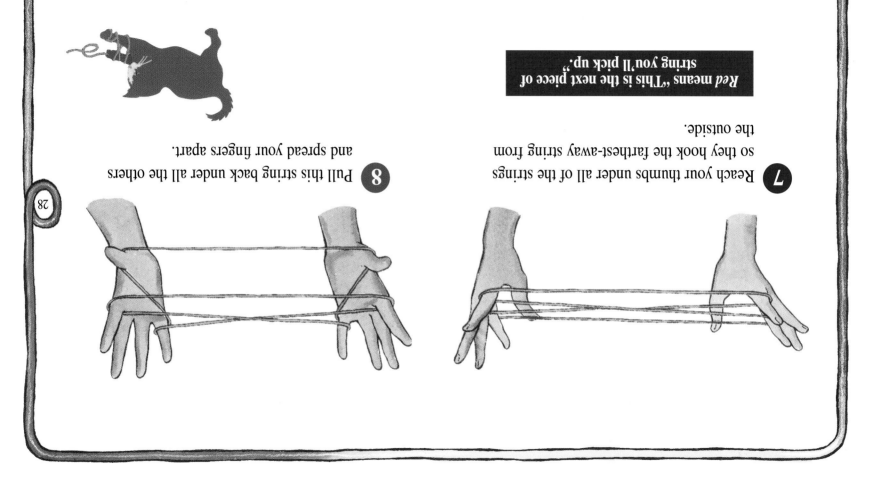

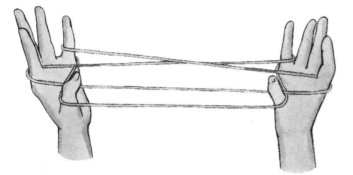

 Now you're going to pick up another loop with your thumbs, but be careful not to drop the loop that already goes around them. Stretch the thumbs over the second string and hook them under the third string (marked in red).

10 Pull this string back. You'll have two loops on each thumb.

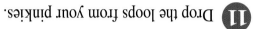
Red means "This is the next piece of string you'll pick up."

11 Drop the loops from your pinkies.

12 Stretch your pinkies over the string that is closest to them and hook them under the next string (we've colored this string red). Look at the picture to be sure you're catching the right string.

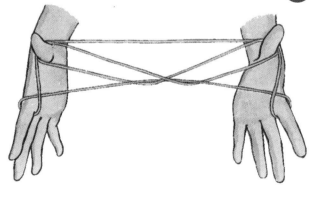

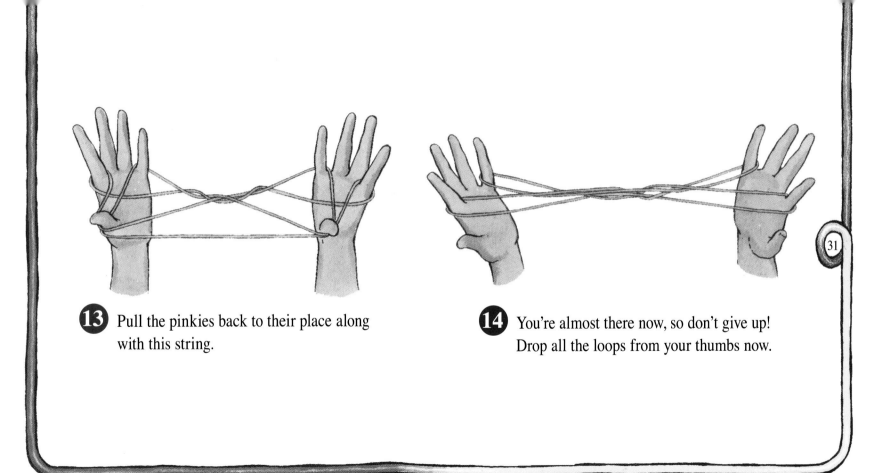

13 Pull the pinkies back to their place along with this string.

14 You're almost there now, so don't give up! Drop all the loops from your thumbs now.

If you stop here, you've made **Cat's Whiskers.**

To keep going . . .

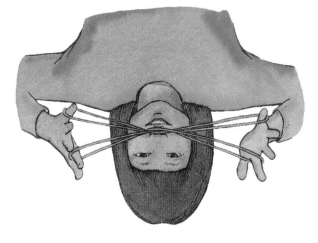

15 Reach your thumbs across the first two strings and hook them up under the third. Pull these strings back toward you.

Red means "This is the next piece of string you'll pick up."

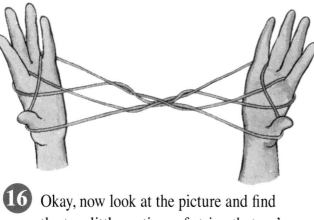

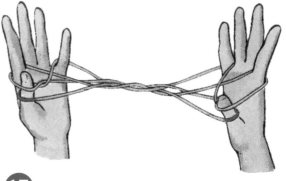

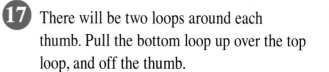

16 Okay, now look at the picture and find the two little sections of string that we've marked with red. Pull each of these sections out and hook it around the nearest thumb. These loops will go around both your first finger and your thumb. Be careful not to drop any loops off of your other fingers while you do this.

17 There will be two loops around each thumb. Pull the bottom loop up over the top loop, and off the thumb.

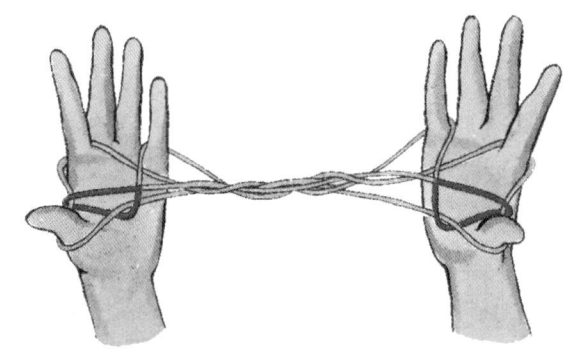

18 Spread your fingers apart. Find the two little triangles we've marked in red.

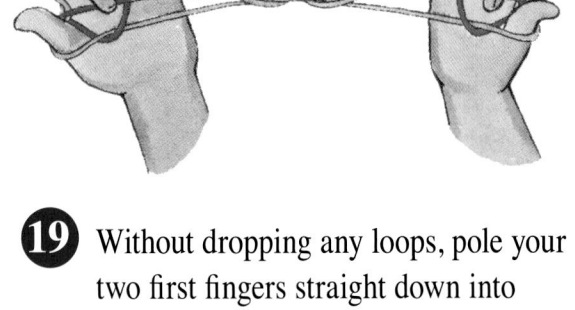

19 Without dropping any loops, pole your two first fingers straight down into these triangles.

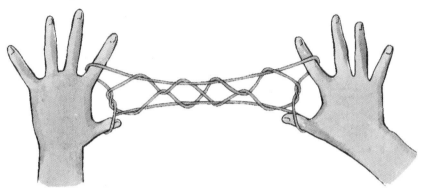

 20 Now turn your palms away from you at the same time that you drop the loops from your pinkies. Spread your fingers apart and you've made **Jacob's Ladder**. This last step is the trickiest. Hardly anyone gets it just right the first time.

Klutz.com • thefolks@klutz.com • 1-800-737-4123

KlutzCertified ▶ KlutzCertified ◎ @KlutzCertified ⏻ KlutzCertified ▶ Klutz

Looking for more goof-proof activities, sneak peeks, and giveaways? Find us online!

Get creative with more from KLUTZ®

Credits

Development
Judith McKibben

Instructional Illustrations
Sara Boore

Book Design & Decorative Illustration
MaryEllen Podgorski

Production
Eileen Stolee
Betty Lowman
Elizabeth Buchanan